WHOLE MIND FACILITATION

D0940245

WHOLE MIND FACILITATION

How to Lead Workshops That Change People, Organizations, and the World

ERIC MEADE

ATIONALLY RECOGNIZED FACILITATOR AND AWARD-WINNING AUTHOR

ILLUSTRATIONS BY LUCINDA LEVINE

Whole Mind Facilitation:
How to Lead Workshops That Change People, Organizations, and the World
Published by Canyon House Press
Superior, CO

Copyright © 2020 Eric Meade. All rights reserved.

No part of this book may be reproduced in any form or by any mechanical means, including information storage and retrieval systems, without permission in writing from the publisher / author, except by a reviewer who may quote passages in a review.

All images, logos, quotes, and trademarks included in this book are subject to use according to trademark and copyright laws of the United States of America.

Publisher's Cataloging-in-Publication Data

Names: Meade, Eric, 1974-, author. | Levine, Lucinda, illustrator.
Title: Whole mind facilitation : how to lead workshops that change people , organizations , and the world / Eric Meade ; Illustrations by Lucinda Levine.
Description: Superior, CO: Canyon House Press, 2020.
Identifiers: ISBN: 978-0-578-67701-9
Subjects: LCSH Meetings. | Business presentations. | Business communication. | Interpersonal communication. | Management. | Leadership. | Organizational change. | BISAC BUSINESS & ECONOMICS / Business Communication / Meetings & Presentations
Classification: LCC HF5718.22 .M43 2020 | DDC 658.452--dc23

Cover design by Victoria Wolf
Cover art by Lucinda Levine

QUANTITY PURCHASES: Schools, companies, professional groups, clubs, and other organizations may qualify for special terms when ordering quantities of this title. For information, email info@canyonhousepress.com.

All rights reserved by Eric Meade and Canyon House Press
This book is printed in the United States of America

For Mom and Dad

Table of Contents

Introduction

"WOW! THAT WAS A REALLY GREAT WORKSHOP! Where did you learn to facilitate like that?"

That's what your clients or colleagues will say to you after you facilitate a workshop using what you will learn in this book. This book is for you – the professional who knows about facilitation and wants to give it a try, but doesn't quite know where to start.

Don't worry about signing up for an expensive facilitation course or certification that offers *the* way to facilitate. Essentially, facilitation is just working with a group of people to help them tackle a difficult problem. With basic knowledge and a little courage, you can do it too!

"Facilitate" comes from the French verb *faciliter*, "to make easier." A great facilitator *makes it easier* for a group of people to do work they need to do. What it requires most of you is your honesty, authenticity, and willingness to stand in front of people with confidence and a commitment to being of service.

And yet, there is a craft to facilitation. A facilitator can take specific steps to make the group's work easier, or take other steps that make their work harder – or even waste their time. You can learn this craft of "do's and don'ts," and you can learn it through this book.

I am writing this book based on my extensive, high-level facilitation experience with clients in the public, private, and non-profit sectors. But I never intended to become an expert facilitator. In fact, I only recently realized that facilitation is a skill one might be really good at. To me, it always just seemed like working with people to solve a problem.

With this experience in mind, I've decided to write down what I have learned about facilitating great workshops. Specifically:

- How to think about a workshop design after that first conversation with a client.
- How to design an agenda and what to consider in the process.
- How to show up in the workshop itself to help the group achieve its objectives.
- How to develop the confidence to stand in front of a group and to be of service to them.
- How to deliver the outputs of a workshop to guide future action.

Let's define our terms before we get started. First, a workshop is a convening of people around a shared interest or issue with the intent of achieving one or more objectives. Workshops differ from meetings in that workshops delve deeper into the relevant issues (internal and external) and seek to achieve an outcome that participants would be unlikely to achieve in the course of their separate day-to-day work or simply through an exchange of information.

A staff meeting, for example, may consist only of reports from leaders about the projects underway within their departments, to which others listen passively. A workshop must go further to create something new through participants' efforts and explorations. Put simply, people "meet" at a meeting, and "work" at a workshop.

For the purposes of this book, a client is anyone who engages you to facilitate a workshop. If you are a consultant, it could be the team leader within an organization who pays you or your firm for your services. If you are an employee, it could be your boss who barks at you one day, "The board wants a strategic planning retreat, and you're going to facilitate it." It may even be your friend who runs a local nonprofit and asks you to facilitate a workshop for her team for free. As a workshop facilitator, you serve the entire group. But when I use the word "client" in this book, I am referring to the individual who convenes the workshop and typically sets or approves its objectives.

———

Great workshops change the world. They do this by changing organizations, and more importantly, by changing people. With today's technologies, people often try to handle important issues through emails and text messages, but with little success. People fire their existing opinions back and forth, often evoking emotional responses that then require additional effort to address. By contrast, great workshops bring people together in a focused, organized way to explore in-depth what is happening and what the group needs to do to move forward. Participants have new conversations, discover new opportunities, or achieve outcomes they would not have believed were possible.

Moribund organizations come back to life at great workshops. Long-standing conflicts get resolved, or at least the parties to the dispute come to understand each other more fully. People learn, grow, and take on new challenges together.

For you as the facilitator, great workshops allow you to be of service to groups that are eager to achieve more than they can without you. And your career will spring forward as others recognize your ability to bring people together to accomplish their shared objectives.

You will facilitate great workshops, and this book will help you do it. First, it will share an overall philosophy of facilitation that has helped me facilitate great workshops for many different kinds of clients. Second, it will equip you with a default "Whole Mind" workshop design, as well as a rubric for tailoring this design to the specific workshop you have been asked to facilitate. Third, it will give you confidence in yourself as a facilitator, even in situations where you genuinely don't know what to do.

If you are a young professional who has never before stood at the front of the room, this book is for you. You will gain the conceptual understanding, tangible skills, and confidence to facilitate at a level far beyond your years of experience.

If you are already an experienced facilitator in your own right, welcome. I hope you will find that this book mirrors the basic truths of facilitation you have discovered for yourself. I also hope that learning about my approach will help you clarify your own, even where we differ.

Please keep in touch to share your facilitation successes and to access additional resources. You can reach me through my website at www.wholemindstrategy.com.

Do we agree on the objectives? Then let's get started.

1

Great Workshops Change People

GREAT WORKSHOPS CHANGE PEOPLE, organizations, and the world. If you have been asked to facilitate a workshop, it is because *someone* wants *something* to change.

Workshops differ from meetings. In meetings, people share information and may even make decisions, but they do not expect to change. As a result, people do not like meetings very much. Over recent years, many have tried to reduce the number of meetings; to turn them into "stand-up" meetings where having everyone on their feet creates a natural pressure to end quickly; or to improve them by having clear agendas, starting on time, or putting off-topic issues in a "parking lot." Even so, the key success criterion for a typical meeting is that it serves its purpose in as little time as possible.

Workshops also differ from training. Training sessions seek to transmit knowledge or skills from the trainer to the audience. Attendees may learn, but rarely do they change their underlying way of thinking. In many cases, training sessions even fail to transmit tangible skills *because* they do not address the underlying ways of thinking that may impede the learning.

At great workshops, people change. Many people look back on a particular workshop as a turning point in their lives or careers. They may point to important insights or opportunities they or their teams discovered. This is the magic you can wield if you hone your craft as a facilitator.

But how does that happen? How do people change? How do people change *together*?

For people to truly change, they must go through a process that engages all three domains of the human mind: *thought, emotion*, and *intuition*.

Thought is our cognitive process that applies a logic we have learned to the facts we have gathered in order to draw conclusions we believe. You can have a good meeting using *thought* alone. You learn new facts from the other participants, and together you test different logics in order to make reasonable, defensible decisions.

Emotion is the bodily and transitory experience of feelings. These feelings predispose us toward different actions. For example, when we feel angry, we tend to argue, attack, or punish. When we feel sad, we tend to withdraw. Further, how we feel shapes what we think, and commits us to logics we have learned that also meet an emotional need by making positive feelings available and keeping negative feelings at bay. Thus, to change what a person thinks, you must first address how they feel.

Intuition is the capacity for awareness of the whole of a situation and of the appropriate actions that one might take. You may have taken actions in the past for which you could offer no rationale; they just felt right. *Intuition* is the space of creative clarity into which we enter once we have released our emotional hold on our current, limited way of thinking. This is where the impossible becomes possible.

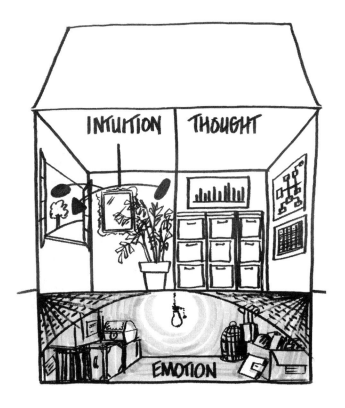

Unfortunately, people cannot get from *thought* to *intuition* directly. You can't walk into a workshop and say, "OK, everyone, be creative!" It doesn't work that way. People can only get from *thought* to *intuition* if they pass through *emotion*.

Imagine a house with two rooms on the first floor (*thought* and *intuition*) and a basement underneath (*emotion*), as shown above. Now imagine that the door between the first-floor rooms only works one way. You can go from *intuition* to *thought*, but you cannot go in the opposite direction. To get from *thought* to *intuition*, you must go through the basement. But the basement is scary. It's dark. You don't know what's down there. But if you make it through, you reach *intuition* on the other side, and that's where people can actually change.

Great workshops start in *thought* to create a common understanding of the problem as currently defined. Then they engage with *emotion* to unpack any limited thinking and deepen the group's motivation to excel together. Then they arrive in *intuition*, where participants discover new insights or develop a multifaceted understanding of the problem. Participants then bring those intuitions back into *thought* in the form of actionable frameworks or plans for the future.

Great workshops begin and end in *thought*, since that's the basis for tangible action in the real world outside the workshop venue. But the two stops in *thought* are very different.

At the beginning of the workshop, *thought* provides a *framework for understanding* based on what is already known and believed. Such a framework (e.g., taxonomies by category, mental maps, and 2x2 matrices) offers common language for discussing the problem, presents the existing facts and data, and ensures through its comprehensiveness that no key aspect of the problem has been overlooked.

At the end of the workshop, however, *thought* provides a *framework for action* that converts the group's discoveries into a construct that will guide them as they move forward. Such a framework (e.g., strategic plans, timelines, and bulleted lists) provides focus for the group's future work by including only those actions that are most critical to success.

A *framework for understanding* provides value by <u>including</u> all relevant information. A *framework for action* provides value by <u>excluding</u> everything but the most critical steps to take. In an ideal scenario, you enter a workshop with a *framework for understanding* (or you build one during the session), and you leave with a (new) *framework for action*.

Early in my facilitation career, I had a client who could not see this difference. I was on the facilitation team for a three-day annual leadership retreat for a large government agency. On the morning of the first day, we introduced a *framework for understanding* developed by another firm supporting the same agency but on a different project. On that afternoon and all of Day Two, we ran small-group exercises organized around that framework. Throughout these exercises, a new framework emerged to capture the most critical steps the agency needed to take in the coming year. This was a *framework for action*; it focused attention and energy on the key things the agency needed to do. In the debrief at the end of Day Two, our team explored with the client the different options for setting up Day Three. Eventually, we came to a decision point: should we organize Day Three's activities around the framework we brought into the workshop, or around the framework that emerged during the small-group exercises? My colleagues and I clearly preferred the latter, but fundamentally the client had to decide. The client decided to stick with the original framework. Why? Because he did not want to be criticized for bringing in the wrong framework in the first place!

Think about that. Great workshops change people. In particular, they change how people think about their problems and about how they might address them. People think in frameworks (whether implicitly or explicitly). In this case, the workshop had successfully prompted participants to identify the key actions they needed to take together, but when it came time to crystallize that thinking, the client could not make the leap with them.

So, in some cases, a participant in a great workshop does *not* change, and if that person is the client, then it can constrain what the other participants can do going forward. I take two lessons from this story. The first is that it may be useful to prepare the client ahead of time by telling them that new ideas and frameworks will likely emerge during the workshop, and that it indicates success rather than failure. The second is that there are limits to what the facilitator can do. Clients are juggling many different organizational dynamics, some of which are not represented in the workshop. The facilitator must ultimately trust that the client is doing the best they can at that time.

In most workshops, the *framework for action* is the prize. It's what awaits you at the end of this journey that starts in *thought*, passes through *emotion*, arrives in *intuition*, and gives you goodies to bring back into the realm of *thought*. It's why the client hired you.

The Whole Mind workshop design shown below can help you attain this price in most situations. It moves from *thought* to *emotion* to *intuition* and back to *thought* through a general sequence of activities that I have found to be remarkably effective across many settings. You will have to decide how to tailor it to your specific circumstances, but we will address that in the next few chapters.

For a more detailed exploration, I have divided this workshop design into two parts:

- An "outbound trip" leading from *thought* through *emotion* into the open space of *intuition*, and
- An "inbound trip" leading from *intuition* back to *thought*.

The metaphor of an "outbound trip" and an "inbound trip" is appropriate because a great workshop is very much a journey of exploration. The group starts in their current thinking, leaves that thinking to enter a larger opportunity space, and brings back what they find there to better understand and address the challenges they face. As the poet T.S. Eliot wrote:

> And the end of all our exploring
> Will be to arrive where we started
> And know the place for the first time.

2

High-Level Design Considerations

GREAT WORKSHOPS ACHIEVE objectives that the group has set out to achieve. But where do these objectives come from?

In some cases, the client will already have a set of objectives in mind. The client is facing an issue that they believe can best be addressed in a workshop format. However, you may need to help the client articulate those objectives in terms that everyone will understand, particularly if the client's thinking is wrapped up in frustration or other negative emotions about the issue at hand.

In other cases, you may need to help the client develop the objectives from scratch. If the workshop occurs on a regular basis (e.g., an annual retreat), then the question may be how best to use the time that has already been scheduled.

Experts have written many books on how to diagnose organizational issues that might be addressed through a workshop or other means. Without presuming to summarize that entire literature, I suggest the following approach to generating workshop objectives if the client expects you to do so.

Deepen your understanding of the group's situation by reviewing relevant materials (e.g., bylaws, strategic plans, and annual reports) and interviewing key stakeholders, including those who will and will not be participating in the workshop. Based on what you learn, work through the following questions to develop the workshop objectives:

1. What is the biggest external issue the group faces? For example, are they facing a budget crunch? Have they neglected important external relationships? Is their business model no longer working?

2. What verb best captures the meaningful progress they could make on that issue during the workshop? Examples include "identify," "explore," "develop," and "decide."

3. What is the biggest internal issue the group faces? For example, is there infighting between departments? Do they lack a clear vision, mission, or strategy? Does their organizational structure hinder collaboration?

4. What verb best captures the meaningful progress they could make on that issue during the workshop?

5. What is the tangible output or outcome they need from this workshop?

The first two objectives will use the verbs to describe the work they will do on their biggest external and internal issues. Sequence these two objectives, either in order of importance or in the order in which they will be accomplished during the workshop. For example:

- To identify at least five potential new business models for further research and development.
- To strengthen our capacity for innovation by building relationships across functions and markets.

The third objective will be to create the tangible output or outcome they need. For example:

- To develop a timeline of research and development activities for the next six months.

Taken together, these three objectives should convey a meaningful scope of work the group can effectively tackle in the workshop. Share them with the client to obtain their feedback and approval.

Once you have set the workshop's objectives, you will need to make several decisions that will set the conditions for their achievement. The first of these is who should attend.

Sometimes the participants are predetermined, as in the case of a board of directors or an executive team. Other times, you can invite a broader set of stakeholders, both internal and external, who will contribute to achieving the objectives.

Specifically, in such cases, I urge clients to be inclusive in inviting all those whose behavior would need to change in order to put the workshop's outcomes fully into practice. This includes those with the authority to make key decisions, those whose opposition might impede progress, those who will do the work of implementation, and those who will be significantly affected by the change. Further, if an organization seeks to strengthen its relationships with external partners, then inviting those partners into its workshop may be a great way to do it.

There is a point, however, at which broad participation in a workshop prevents the group from reaching any meaningful agreement. Thus, it may make more sense to form a movement of those with the passion, energy, and resources to bring about a significant positive change, without first getting everyone's input. In such cases, an initial smaller workshop (e.g., of eight to ten key players) could lead to larger workshops with a broader set of stakeholders after key decisions have been made.

Once you have identified the participants, ask them to "save the date" you have in mind for the workshop. It can be challenging to find a date that works for a large group of busy people, so get the workshop on their calendars as early as possible.

The next issue to address is where to hold the workshop. This is a significant enough success factor for your facilitation that you should get involved in the venue planning as soon as the client engages you to do the facilitation.

The client may already have decided on a venue before asking you to facilitate, particularly if the workshop has been on the calendar for a long time. In the worst case, the client has already booked a boardroom in a conference hotel with a fixed wooden table, low ceilings, poor lighting, and no windows. That kind of venue may force you to lower your expectations for the workshop; in fact, I have trouble even using the word "workshop" to describe a gathering in such a location.

In the best-case scenario, you can get involved in selecting the venue early on, and you can suggest venues consistent with the workshop's objectives. For example, I once facilitated a leadership retreat for a community-wide health improvement initiative in Memphis, Tennessee. The group had initially planned to hold the retreat in the "community room" at one of the participating organizations, a health clinic for the uninsured. That is where they *always* met. I knew this retreat had to be different from their typical meetings, so the venue had to change as well. On my initial trip to Memphis to conduct participant interviews, I drove past the Children's Museum of Memphis and heard children running around outside it. It struck me as a fantastic place to hold a retreat focused on the future of the community's health. We'd be able to hear the future all around us! To my delight, I succeeded in getting the client to reserve the "blue birthday room" at the museum. I'm confident that the retreat turned out much better than if we had been in the community room where they normally met.

Look for a venue with an open room with movable furniture and enough space for your number of participants to move around freely, walls where you can post flip-chart paper and

Post-it notes, and windows providing natural light. Ideally, the space would have a pleasant view and direct access to the outdoors, weather permitting.

Also consider that your participants may have apparent or non-apparent disabilities, or reduced mobility due to age or injury. Always choose venues that comply with the Americans with Disabilities Act (ADA) or its equivalent in your country, for example, by having ramp or elevator access to the room where the workshop will occur, as well as to restrooms, cafeterias, and any other places participants are likely to go. Pay attention to things like lighting and background noise, so everyone can see and hear clearly. If you ignore these issues, some participants may find it difficult or even impossible to engage in the workshop activities, and you will lose the benefit of their contributions. When possible, ask participants ahead of time what they need in order to participate fully, and plan accordingly.

Once you have decided on a venue, ask the client to send the full invitation out to participants. This should include the purpose of the workshop; the date, time, and location; directions for transportation and parking; information about food that will be provided (and an inquiry into dietary restrictions, if appropriate); as well as the attire they should wear. In general, set the dress code to be as casual as possible given the participants' organizational culture or cultures. This helps create a relaxed environment where people feel freer to speak their minds.

As for setting up the room, I prefer a circle of movable chairs (one for me and one for each participant) and <u>no tables</u>. I can accept a table or two along the walls for snacks, coffee, and supplies. As you will see in the following chapters, I like to have three flip-charts for my favorite activities, but I can get by with only one if necessary.

If I plan to use slides for a presentation, I ask for a screen and projector. In that case, I open the circle of chairs to face the screen, recognizing that some participants may need to turn their bodies or chairs a little during the presentation. (I prefer to present using only a flip-chart since it feels more interactive and I can adjust the presentation as I go, but more complicated content requires slides.)

I seat everyone in the circle, even junior staff, since it feels awkward to me to be watched by people sitting outside the circle. In general, if you cannot sit in the circle, then you should not be in the room. The only exception to this rule is a junior staff member whose only role in the workshop is to take notes. But as you will learn later, I see no great need for note-takers.

Simply suggesting that tables be removed from the room may already mark you as a maverick, and some clients may resist. They may fear that participants will find it odd sitting in a circle of chairs. But I have found that with a little confidence and humor ("This is *not* an intervention!"), I can get participants comfortable with the setup.

Some clients resist removing the tables because they know participants will want to have their computers in front of them. Ironically, these are often the same clients who complain that workshop participants are on their computers and not engaging in the discussions!

Seating participants in a circle of chairs with no tables does more than get rid of the computers; it immediately shifts the energy of the workshop. It clears the channels for nonverbal communication among participants; they engage in the workshop not as titled roles in an organizational chart but rather as real-life human beings. This vastly increases your odds of accessing their *emotion* and *intuition.*

If the work you have planned only requires *thought,* as in the case of bylaw revisions, for example, then by all means seat participants at tables. You may also need round tables (seating no more than eight people) for some small-group activities, but hopefully your venue *also* has space for a circle of chairs where participants can sit for full-group conversations. The image below shows a range of suitable room setups.

As noted, removing the tables and setting up a circle of chairs immediately shifts the energy of the workshop. Fortunately, it is never too late to do it. Recently, a client hired me at the last minute to facilitate a workshop at the Army and Navy Club in Washington, D.C. When I arrived, I found a long, ornate room with eight-foot ceilings and an imposing chandelier in the middle. A U-shaped table ran the length of the room. I did what I could: I prevailed upon the client to have the venue staff remove the tables and set up at least an oval of chairs. But the chandelier was there to stay!

Take a risk. Remove the tables and set up a circle of chairs.

Before we address the workshop agenda, let's consider a few other elements.

GIVE PARTICIPANTS THE BREAKS THEY NEED

Throughout the workshop, participants will need breaks. A U.S. Air Force psychiatrist with whom I once worked was adamant that workshops should alternate between forty-five-minute sessions (the length of the average human attention span) and twenty-minute breaks (enough time to use the restroom, make a phone call, refill your coffee, and catch up with a colleague). If sessions are any longer or breaks any shorter, my friend argued, participants cannot engage fully.

Some clients, when you suggest that ratio of sessions to breaks, might exclaim, "If we're spending that much time on breaks, what do I need *you* for?!"

But this ignores the value of breaks. No matter how successful the workshop, participants *also* consistently note the networking that occurs during breaks as among the most valuable aspects of the event. Peers chatting over breaks undoubtedly discover areas where they can usefully combine their efforts. Breaks also create a space for participants to talk with trusted colleagues and test ideas that they are not yet willing to say in front of the whole group. Further, the personal relationship-building that occurs over breaks typically proves valuable both in its own right and for the workshop's purposes.

As a facilitator, you need breaks too! Breaks allow you to set up for the next activity, use the restroom, mingle with participants, check in with the client and key participants, and get a sense of the group's energy and focus as they talk among themselves.

Respect the breaks. At a bare minimum, give participants (and yourself) a fifteen-minute break after one hour and fifteen minutes of work that includes some movement or small-group work, and more frequently if the work consists of presentations or full-group discussions.

If food will be served during breaks, encourage clients to choose healthy snacks and beverages. Sugary items like dough-nuts and soda may give participants a short burst of energy, but will leave them dragging later on. Healthy items like fruit, nuts, granola bars, water, and iced tea will keep participants energized, hydrated, and able to perform at their best.

CREATE A RHYTHM OF INDIVIDUAL, SMALL-GROUP, AND FULL-GROUP ACTIVITIES

Great workshops offer participants a mix of activities to accommodate different learning styles, work styles, personalities, and tasks. Create a rhythm that alternates among the various options at your disposal. I typically use a brief series of full-group activities to get everyone oriented to the process, and then alternate between small groups for brainstorming and exploration, and the full group for synthesis and prioritization.

Include time for individual work. I call this "protecting the introverts," since many introverts need time to themselves to figure out what they think before they can share it with others. If you lead the entire workshop as a full-group discussion, you will lose a good deal of what they might otherwise contribute.

When you set up small groups, give thought to how you will put people together. Sometimes it is useful to group people with similar perspectives, while at other times, it works better to set up each group as a microcosm of the full group.

In their facilitation classic, *Don't Just Do Something, Stand There!*, Marvin Weisbord and Sandra Janoff write about the psychological dynamic of differentiation and integration. The key point is that members of a group must first "differentiate" – that is, express their unique perspective – before they can "integrate" by coming to consensus or agreement.

Help participants differentiate early in the workshop by putting them in groups with others who share their opinion. They will feel validated as they hear others express perspectives similar to their own, and together they can craft a way of expressing their shared perspective to the full group. Later in the workshop, form groups with a variety of perspectives so that the ideas and opportunities they generate address the interests of the full group rather than only those of a particular perspective. If you create an alternating rhythm throughout the small-group work between these two models, participants will sustain their feelings of validation while contributing to discussions that ultimately serve the whole.

After small-group activities, allow the groups to report out the highlights of their discussions, but do not assume the full group needs to hear everything they discussed. It is often useful *not* to report out at length, and instead to let the ideas that emerged in small groups percolate for a while to see what happens to them organically.

SCHEDULE ACTIVITIES WITH THE TIME OF DAY IN MIND

People excel in different activities at different times of the day. I almost always schedule the creative activities in a workshop in the morning and use the afternoons for presentations, analysis, and planning. I find that most people (including me) do their most creative work in the morning when they are fresh and alert.

If a client asks you to facilitate a 1½-day workshop, do not assume that it needs to be all of the first day and half of the second. In some cases, this makes sense – e.g., a strategic planning retreat with exploration in the morning, high-level planning in the afternoon, and detailed activity planning the following morning once everyone has had a night to "sleep on" the priorities identified on Day One.

In other cases, however, it may make more sense to start on the afternoon of Day One with presentations on context and methodology, get participants doing small-group creative work the next morning, and then finish up with the planning that afternoon. Again, the common feature of both designs is that participants do the creative work in the morning.

Another planning consideration is that many people fall into a "food coma" right after lunch. With most of their blood in their stomachs (and not in their brains), they find it difficult to engage as fully as they did in the morning. If the client wants the workshop to include a presentation that is not directly relevant to the workshop's outcomes, I schedule it for right after lunch. If not, then I try to schedule small-group work, preferably something that gets people moving, and I give them a break after only about forty-five minutes. When they come back from that break, they are typically ready to engage fully once more.

HAVE THE GROUP DOCUMENT THEIR OWN WORK

As part of your workshop design, decide how participants will capture the highlights of their discussions and activities as

INITIATIVE	GOALS	ACTIONS	KEY MILESTONES
1.			
2.			
3.			

they go. No one wants to sift through fifty pages of meticulous notes to find the few kernels that will drive the group forward once the workshop ends, so consider dispensing with note-taking altogether. Instead, develop exercise templates for saving the ideas and information worth collecting, and develop a strategy for capturing highlights from full-group discussions on flipcharts that can be compiled as a workshop summary.

Most importantly, these templates should capture the actions the group plans to take after the workshop and any information necessary for them to do so. For example, if a small group works on an initiative to build relationships with external stakeholders, have a template that captures the highest-priority stakeholders, the potential benefits of the relationships, and any partners who can help by making introductions. Essentially, have the group capture enough information that another group could pick up wherever they leave off.

In some cases, it is useful to capture information from activities where the group looks at its own past, especially when they create a shared understanding that did not exist before. This could be a timeline of the group's history or an exercise to take stock of how its various projects are going. In these cases, a facilitator can serve a group by helping them retain this information for future use.

In most cases, it makes sense for someone to write up a summary of the workshop to remind participants what they decided and to give those who did not attend some context for the decisions. In his classic, *Million Dollar Consulting*, Alan Weiss urges against writing the workshop summary for the client if this is not a core part of your business. In my case, I prefer to write the summary myself since it allows me to write the history, highlighting the workshop's most useful aspects and documenting the *framework for action* while leaving out the play-by-play detail that makes many workshop summaries so painful to read. As my mentor Jonathan Peck taught me, "The report should be even better than the workshop."

Now that we've dispensed with those overall design considerations, let's get into what you will be facilitating. What activities should you plan, and how should you move participants through the activities?

GRAPHIC RECORDING

Consider hiring a graphic recorder to capture the workshop's key ideas in visual artwork that can be used not just in a workshop summary but also in the group's other communications. Graphic recorders draw graphics in real time during the workshop discussions, giving the graphics an organic quality.

Graphic recording works particularly well in a Whole Mind workshop since the Whole Mind approach explicitly engages emotion and intuition, both of which are better expressed artistically than in a simple list of bulleted points. Further, when viewed long after the workshop has ended, these graphics trigger an emotional memory that brings back all the richness of the conversations on which they were based.

At the very least, participants consistently enjoy having a graphic recorder at the meeting. There is something special about watching someone transform your conversation into a work of art.

This book's illustrator, Lucinda Levine, is an accomplished graphic recorder. Visit her at www.Inkquiryvisuals.com.

3

The Outbound Trip: From *Thought* to *Emotion* to *Intuition*

TO USE THE WHOLE MIND WORKSHOP design effectively, you will need to make a few decisions to tailor the design to help your group of participants achieve the workshop's objectives. This chapter will present options for each step on the "outbound trip," and the considerations that would lead you to choose each one. You can also refer to the design flowchart on the following two pages.

In this first part of the workshop, the group:

- Starts in *thought* by orienting themselves to the objectives, agenda, agreements, and topic for the day,
- Accesses their *emotion* through introductions, grounding, and small-group discussions, and
- Arrives in *intuition* where they develop a more holistic understanding and likely find intimations of how to proceed.

Design Flowchart for the "Outbound Trip"

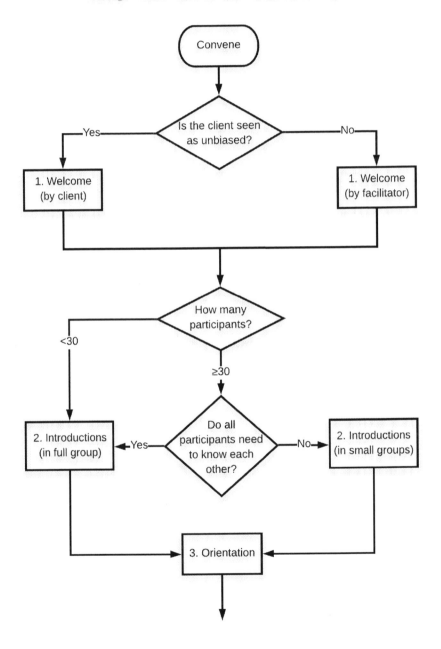

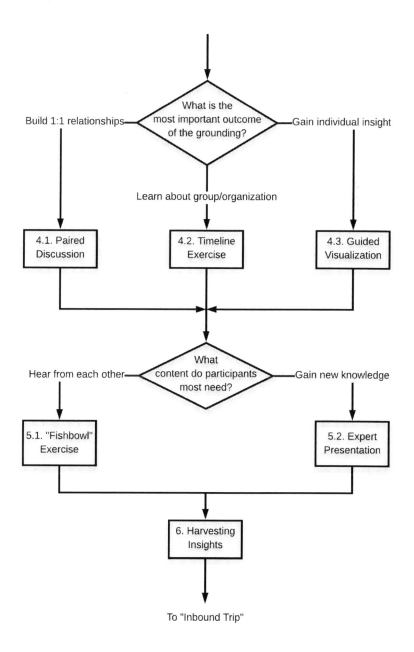

On the "inbound trip" that follows, the group translates these intimations into clear *frameworks for action* that will guide them forward. We will address this in the next chapter.

PREPARING, ARRIVING, AND SETTING UP

We will start our journey at the moment you wake up on the day of the workshop. One of the first questions you will need to answer as a facilitator is: what should I wear?

As I noted earlier, I like to ask participants to dress as casually as their culture allows. Then I like to dress at the formal end of the range I expect them to wear. For example, if they normally wear suits, I might ask them to wear business casual (e.g., dress shirt and chinos) to the workshop, and then I may wear a dress shirt, chinos, and a sport coat. I also like to wear an item or two that conveys confidence, power, and authority, like a nice pair of leather dress boots.

Wherever possible, I avoid wearing a suit and tie, since I find it a little more difficult to be fully present with fancy clothes on and a piece of silk wrapped tightly around my neck. So in the vast majority of situations, I suggest prioritizing your physical comfort over rote conformity with any dress code provided by a client. Further, plenty of ways exist to "dress up" a comfortable but less formal outfit, for example, by wearing nice leather shoes or a pocket square.

You also may want to communicate something specific with your clothing. Match your clothes to the culture of the group you are facilitating, for example, by wearing cowboy boots in a rural setting or a navy blazer in a corporate gathering. To signal that this workshop is different from the meetings they typically attend, wear something tasteful that they would never wear – e.g., burgundy pants, white jeans, or a jean jacket.

Of course, I have written this from my perspective as a man with a relatively traditional style of dress. Because women have many more dress options, women facilitators may need to spend even more time planning their outfits. For this reason, I have asked my good friend and colleague Emily Oehler – a master facilitator in her own right – to share her thoughts on how a woman facilitator can dress for success.

———

Over the past decade, Eric and I have facilitated many workshops together. When we work in the same space, I am reminded of the gifts we each offer the participants and each other as partners in the process. I'm fairly certain, however, that I put a little more thought into what I wear – not because he does not look nice, but because I am very aware of my physical presence as a woman.

In selecting an outfit, I think about authority, comfort, practicality, and emotion.

- *Does the outfit add to or detract from my authority in the room? Is it too formal or too casual compared to what the participants are wearing?*

- *Am I comfortable? Does the outfit move with my body or restrict my movements?*
- *Is my attire practical for the work to be done? Specifically, does it have pockets for pens, markers, and Post-it notes? Does it cover all my parts whether I'm standing up, bending down, or squatting to write on the lower half of a flip-chart?*
- *Does it lift my mood and give me the confidence required to take smart facilitation risks?*

While I do not need to be a subject matter expert at every workshop I facilitate, I do need to command attention in a room of senior leaders with plenty of MDs, PhDs, and MBAs after their names. What I wear helps or hinders this. I have two "go-to" outfits: a pantsuit with a cotton shirt, or capri pants with a jacket or sweater. Both meet all my criteria for dressing for facilitation success.

Whatever you wear, avoid the following items that will likely make you stand out more than the participants:

- *Lacy undergarments that show through your clothes or have exposed straps*
- *Clingy silk blouses*
- *Dangly earrings or noisy jewelry*
- *Body-conscious materials*
- *Bold, colorful prints*

And lastly, hair. I tend to move around as a facilitator and I like to make direct eye contact with participants. I have found that I do both better if my hair is pulled back. That way, it doesn't constantly drop into my face and I am not fidgeting with it, which participants might perceive as nervousness.

At the end of the day, you will know the right outfit when you put it on. It will feel like a protective suit of self-confidence, and it will bring a smile to your face.

One more thing before you leave home: Grab any facilitation materials you will need at the workshop that the client is not providing. For me, that usually means a set of Sharpie chisel-tip permanent markers and a few pads of six-by-eight-inch Post-it notes, at a minimum.

Arrive at the workshop venue at least one hour before participants will arrive. Once there, take care of the logistical details that will help participants feel truly welcome when they arrive. In most cases, the client or their staff will handle many of these, but you should check that everything is ready to go. For example, are there signs directing participants from the building entrance to the room? Are the nametags (if planned) set out for participants to pick up as they come in?

Touch base with the client if they have already arrived. Remind them of anything you have asked them to do. For example, make sure they have thought through what they will say as they welcome the group. Ask if there is any last-minute information you should know about the workshop or the participants.

Then set up for your facilitation, and in particular, the orientation you will provide shortly after the workshop begins. On three separate flip-chart pages, write the workshop's objectives, agenda, and agreements (meeting norms). Hang the pages on the walls, or leave them on three different easels if you have that many.

The objectives come directly from the agenda you built and confirmed with the client in advance, and that participants themselves may have already seen. You can abridge the agenda when you transfer it to a flip-chart to make it fit or to remove unnecessary details. Also, you can leave off the specific times from the agenda if you want to convey to participants that you will be flexible in your management of time. As for agreements, I have a default set I use in most workshops; you will find these in the orientation discussion later in this chapter.

With logistics in place and these three flip-chart pages hanging in visible spots, you can take a short break as participants arrive, mingle, and get settled. How you use this time is entirely up to you. A former colleague of mine, an extravert, spends this time introducing himself to every participant as they enter the room. As an introvert, I like to use this time to collect my thoughts and observe the participants from afar. I greet participants I already know, but otherwise, I am happy to wait to be introduced by the client. If I have anything left to prepare, I try to do it calmly and professionally to convey confidence and professionalism.

1. WELCOME

At the appointed time, summon participants from the coffee table or their small-group chit-chat and have them take their seats. The welcome then convenes them and starts the workshop. In most cases, ask the client to welcome participants and offer a few sentences on their hopes for the day. It is their meeting, so by giving the welcome, they accept ownership – with the others present – of the day's outcomes. They might also briefly say how they know you, the facilitator, and that they will give serious consideration (if they are in a position of authority over the group) to whatever emerges from the discussions.

In most cases, avoid doing the welcome yourself since it may convey a lack of commitment on the client's part to the workshop, to you, or to the outcomes that will be achieved. However, in cases where there is animosity between the client and the other participants, having the client do the welcome may trigger cynicism, whereas doing the welcome yourself may establish the workshop as "neutral territory."

2. INTRODUCTIONS

Most people do not like sitting in a workshop for long without speaking; they soon shift into a passive "receive-only" mode, listening to what the "teacher" has to say. Introductions are a great way to get participants talking early on, even if they already know each other.

But poorly executed, introductions can use up a lot of time and energy. Many workshops have gone awry because the facilitator asked a group of twenty or more participants to "take a few minutes to introduce yourself." If "a few" means three, then you just burned an hour. Further, few people understand how quickly three minutes go by, so most take five, while others talk until someone cuts them off.

Introductions should take no more than fifteen minutes, or up to twenty minutes in larger groups where participants need to know one another. Schedule that much time, and do not let it go any longer.

In a workshop of fewer than thirty participants where people do not know each other as well as they would like, ask participants to take turns introducing themselves, but give them three specific questions, such as:

- *What is your name? How long have you been with the organization? What would you like to get out of today?* This is a safe option since it addresses the workshop itself, but the answers can get stale if participants do not really know what the workshop is about, or if they are unenthusiastic about its potential.
- *What is your name? What is your title, role, or organization? What is your connection to [the workshop topic]?* This usually surfaces surprising information about people beyond their organizational relationship with the topic, so it brings in personal information while staying focused on the workshop itself.
- *What is your name? What is your title or role? What are your thoughts and feelings right now?* This is a bit deeper, and thus more risky, but a participant can always answer with a safe feeling like "tired" or "curious."

Avoid clever icebreaker questions like, "What's something everyone in this room would be surprised to learn about you?" or "If you were an ice cream flavor, what flavor would you be, and why?" Such questions present participants with the cognitive task of saying something that fits your framework rather than a genuine opportunity to express what is true for them in their own words. Thus they shift participants' attention from each other to the facilitator, and in most cases, the cynicism triggered among those who despise such questions outweighs the delight of those who love them. But clever questions aside, the specific question you ask is less important than the fact that you are giving participants an opportunity to speak.

Since this is the first time participants are speaking, be sure to establish yourself as a facilitator by preventing anyone from going on for too long. The group wants to know that you will protect them from having their time wasted, even by one of their own.

If there are thirty or more participants and the workshop's success does not depend on everyone knowing everyone else, invite participants to introduce themselves within small groups, especially if they will work in those groups throughout the day. Calculate the time allowed based on one to two minutes per person, and then let the groups manage time for themselves.

If participants already feel comfortable with one another, consider taking the introductions deeper by combining them with the "grounding." This will also save you time. (The grounding invites participants to shift from "getting here" to "being here" and to tap more fully into the domains of *emotion* and *intuition*.) For example, ask participants to check in using the PIES framework, sharing what is happening for them physically, intellectually, emotionally, and spiritually. The word "spiritual" may put some people off, but in my experience, those who do not consider themselves spiritual will simply say so, or they will interpret the word in a way that works for them.

HANDLING PARTICIPANTS
WHO TALK TOO MUCH

The group expects you to prevent their time from being wasted by a fellow participant who rambles on about a topic that does not serve the group. Here is how you do it:

- Avoid handing a microphone over to a participant. If you have to, then stand near them while they talk, and when you are ready for them to stop talking, reach out for them to give it back to you. Never allow participants to pass the microphone among themselves.
- If seated, stand up. This puts you in everyone's field of view and reminds the speaker who is going on too long that you are in charge.
- Move toward the speaker. At first, this might be very subtle – walking from twenty to sixteen paces away. If they keep talking, move closer. Even the most self-absorbed participant will likely stop talking once you are standing right beside them.

If you need to cut the speaker off, do so gently. For example, say, "Thank you for your comments. I'm going to ask that you end there so we can hear from everyone." If they have established a pattern of this behavior, address it privately during a break.

3. ORIENTATION

This is your chance to establish a structure for the workshop by presenting the objectives, agenda, and agreements you wrote on flip-chart pages when you first arrived.

You developed the objectives in Chapter 2 and you are designing the agenda in this chapter and the next. The agreements are just behavioral norms likely to make the workshop a success.

Over time, you will develop your own default set of agreements, but those listed here will work well enough when you are just starting out. The image on the opposite page shows the agreements, and the italicized text below offers language you can use to present them.

Respect the agenda and time limits. I see the agenda as a forecast of the "expectable future," so in all likelihood, it will change as we go. But if I say, "Take a fifteen-minute break," please do come back within fifteen minutes so we can get started again.

Turn off things that make noise without notice. Please turn off your computers, phones, and anything else that could distract you or your colleagues.

Be fully present during retreat activities and discussions. Today is a great opportunity to spend time together and to do the work that we need to do together. So please make the most of that time by being fully present to the things happening in this room.

Listen to understand, not to respond. We'll know you're listening to respond if you immediately jump in once someone

else is done talking. Actually, this means that you weren't really listening; you were planning what you were going to say next. Listening to understand means that you are fully engaged in what the other person is saying, and when they're finished, you pause to process what they've said. Then if you have something you'd like to say, you're welcome to share it. Also, be curious about perspectives other than your own, and try to see the logic in other views.

Speak to be understood. Specifically:

- *Use "I" statements, not "you" statements. That means speak in terms of your own experience, like, "I think," "I feel," "I do," and not "You think," "You feel," "You do."*
- *W.A.I.T. stands for "why am I talking?" If you find yourself going around and around, saying the same things over and over, maybe it's time to let someone else have a chance to talk.*
- *Avoid or explain jargon. Don't assume that everyone knows the terms and abbreviations you're using. Likewise, if someone uses a term you don't know, ask what it means. There's no expectation that the people in this room know everything.*

I particularly like "W.A.I.T.," which I learned from my friends at Washington, D.C.-based nonprofit CommonHealth ACTION. It nearly always gets a chuckle from participants, and it's always good to start with a laugh.

Most workshops address topics that are not public information, such as business performance, budget planning, or interpersonal conflicts. If this is the case, include an agreement on confidentiality. Where the topic is not confidential per se, but the conversations will be more candid than they might be in a public forum, invoke the "Chatham House Rule." It means participants are free to use the information they hear at a workshop but agree not to reveal the identity or affiliation of the speaker or any other participant.

Also, remember that you, as the facilitator, will hear information to which you would not be privy outside your facilitator role. Respect that the participants are welcoming you into their "inner chambers" and protect the privacy and confidentiality of what you hear there. Make a personal commitment not to use that information for personal gain in the future.

If there is broad agreement within the group about the workshop's objectives and no large power differentials among the participants, add another agreement: "It's YOUR meeting." This agreement clarifies responsibilities for the workshop's outcomes. Remember, you can facilitate the group's work, but you cannot do it for them. I tell groups that if the exercise I have them doing is not meeting their needs, they should tell me. Then we'll do something else.

Making this agreement explicit serves two purposes. First, it reminds participants that they hold ultimate responsibility for the workshop's success. Second, it creates psychological distance between you and the agenda you so painstakingly designed, so that you can more easily deviate from it if doing so would better serve the group.

After you present each page (objectives, agenda, and agreements), solicit agreement from the group by asking each participant to give a "thumbs-up." For agreements, ask if anyone has another agreement to recommend that has worked well in other workshops they have attended in the past. At this point, someone often suggests adding, "Have fun!" Modify the flip-chart if there is consensus among the group.

In this presentation, I have placed the introductions before the orientation, but you could do them in the opposite order. By doing the orientation first, you get people "on the same page," and you get mobile phones set to "silent" before participants start talking. This may be appropriate in groups that are likely to push the boundaries in terms of behavior, or that are so big that introductions will take longer than average. By doing the introductions first, you send the message that hearing from participants is your top priority, but at the risk that a phone will ring while someone is talking. Also, by force of habit, some clients may move directly from their welcome to introductions, even if that is not what you planned with them beforehand.

4. GROUNDING

This step invites participants to shift from "getting here" to "being here," to become fully present in the room, which allows them to bring not just their *thought* but also their *emotion* and *intuition* to bear on the problem at hand. Many workshops and meetings ignore this step and end up stuck in *thought* as a result. Many approaches will work as a grounding so long as they demonstrate respect for the group. As with introductions, trite icebreaker questions do not.

Some groups may not be open to doing a grounding, in which case you can skip it. But if the resistance is tentative, based on unfamiliarity rather than unpalatability, then take a risk and do it. The more resistant the group, the more they likely have to gain.

4.1 Paired Discussion

Invite participants to reflect on a question like the following for a few minutes, and then pair up to discuss.

- *What past accomplishment [in this field or at this organization] gives you the most pride?*
- *What would a surprising level of success look like for this workshop?*

Follow the energy of the paired discussions; allow at least a couple minutes for each participant to share, remind them to switch who is speaking, and then bring the group back together once the discussions are slowing or shifting to more mundane topics. Facilitate a brief, full-group sharing of their reflections.

Some facilitators use the question, "What led you to this kind of work?" which can work in some contexts and not in others. While it seems harmless, it may lead people to share past traumas for which the group may not be prepared, particularly in "helper" professions like psychology, healthcare, or social work. For this reason, I prefer questions that do not put participants on the spot to share more than they would like.

4.2 Timeline Exercise

This exercise comes from Marvin Weisbord and Sandra Janoff's "Future Search" process, which is a three-day format for future-focused action planning by diverse stakeholders across an entire system.[1] It occurs early in that process, just as I am suggesting you use it early on in your workshop.

Hang three long sheets of "butcher block" or craft paper (at least six feet, but preferably eight to ten feet) on the walls, or if necessary, position them on tables or the floor. Put five to ten markers near each one. (Test the markers and paper ahead of time to ensure the ink won't bleed through onto the walls, tables, or carpet!)

Each sheet will become a timeline looking back twenty to thirty years. Weisbord and Janoff use thirty years as a default, but I prefer to look back twenty years when working with groups of people predominantly in their twenties and thirties. Prepare each sheet with a timeline, year marks, and a label and graphic indicating which timeline it is, as shown on the next page.

One timeline captures events and trends at a global scale (affecting all sectors and industries), the second timeline captures events and trends at an institutional and/or sectoral level, and the third timeline captures them at the personal level – births, marriages, divorces, graduations, new jobs, etc.

Invite participants to roam around the room, adding content to all three timelines. Encourage everyone to contribute

---

1. I have modified the exercise slightly. See *Future Search: Getting the Whole System in the Room for Vision, Commitment, and Action* by Weisbord and Janoff for the original version.

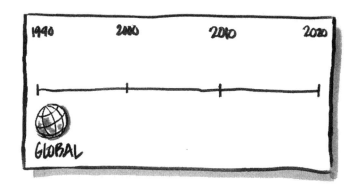

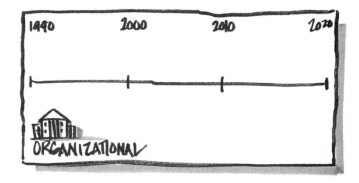

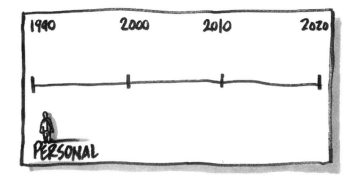

something to each timeline. You may have to reiterate that you really do want people to put events from their own lives on the "personal" timeline.

Once the timelines have sufficient content, and fewer people are still writing, form participants into three groups. Assign one group to each timeline and give them ten to fifteen minutes to answer these two questions:

- *What is the story told by your timeline?*
- *What are the implications of this story for the work we'll be doing together today and beyond?*

Ask each group to share their answers with the full group, in order of global, institutional, and personal. Lead a brief discussion of what they said.

This exercise serves several functions. It creates a shared understanding of the past, which newer entrants to the group may not know. It puts people in a position of learning as they hear what events other participants view as significant and as they work with others to find out when a certain event actually occurred. It helps pull people out of their own perspectives by seeing their efforts along a longer timeline of activity. It welcomes them as whole people by implying that their personal experiences are relevant to the group's work together. Lastly, it highlights important shifts in their strategic context that may point to opportunities they have yet to consider.

4.3 Guided Visualization

If you're willing to take a bit of a risk, invite the group into a different mental space by leading them through a guided visualization. Like a meditation, this involves having them close their eyes, take deep breaths, and let your words guide their thoughts.

I provide two scripts that illustrate how I have effectively used guided visualization for two different purposes: exploring the future and centering on the group's purpose.

Whether you use all or part of a script provided here or you use a script you find elsewhere, be brave enough to stand in the unique space you created for participants. It is better to be seen as a facilitator who takes risks that sometimes don't work out than to be seen as a facilitator who backs away from a technique before it has run its course. Further, the benefit of an activity may not be evident or appreciated until much later, so be patient.

Tell the group that there is such a thing as "relaxation-induced anxiety," so if they feel uncomfortable with the exercise, they are welcome to do whatever they need to do to stay safe, which could include keeping their eyes open, not participating, or even leaving the room temporarily.

Both scripts end with instructions for participants to write notes using a pen and paper that they have placed on the floor in front of them before the visualization. These notes will help them remember what they experienced during the visualization, once they start discussing it with a partner later on. Remember to have them prepare these materials ahead of time so that their experience is not disrupted by having to look for a pen and paper, or – even better – have these in their chair when they arrive.

I have used the following script in workshops with health-care leaders. It has a health focus, but you could easily adapt the script to explore the future of whatever field your workshop addresses.

Visualizing the Future

I invite you to sit comfortably in your chairs with your feet on the ground, shoulder-width apart, and take a few deep breaths. As you inhale, imagine you are breathing in the purest air you can imagine, and you feel clean and refreshed. As you exhale, breathe out any stress or anxiety you may be feeling.

Now imagine you start to feel very light, so light that you feel yourself lifting out of your body. Imagine that you are floating upward, that you pass through the ceiling of this room, and that you find yourself floating upward until you are floating through the sky.

Soon you discover that you are floating not only through space but also through time, and you can see the world below you changing. You start to descend, and when you land back on the ground, you discover that it is the year _____.

Walk around to see what life is like now. What does the landscape look like? Where do people live and work? How do they spend their time? What type of work do they do? What do you see that is different from the year you came from?

Now find someone who is remarkably healthy. Ask them what life is like for them. How have they achieved that level of health? What insights do they have to offer for our workshop today? Ask them any other questions you have for them, and when you're finished speaking with them, thank them and say goodbye.

Now find someone who is struggling health-wise. Ask them what life is like for them. What is holding them back from achieving better health? What insights do they have to offer for our workshop today? Ask them any other questions you have for them, and when you're finished speaking with them, thank them and say goodbye.

Take a look at anything else you'd like to see in this future. What would you like to remember when you come back to your own time?

When you're ready, allow yourself to float back up into the sky and feel yourself moving through the air. You see the world below you shifting back to what you have known. You start to see structures and landscapes that look familiar, and you feel yourself descending toward this building, this room. As you get closer, you pass through the ceiling and you ease yourself back into your body, which is in the chair in this room.

Take a moment to get settled, and when you're ready, I invite you to open your eyes, take the pen and paper on the floor in front of you, and jot down a few notes about the experience you've just had.

The following script follows the same basic structure but focuses not on the future but on the higher purpose that is already served by the group's work together. This visualization could be used in most workshops if you feel the group will accept it.

Visualizing the Purpose

I invite you to sit comfortably in your chairs with your feet on the ground, shoulder-width apart, and take a few deep breaths. As you inhale, imagine you are breathing in the purest air you can imagine, and you feel clean and refreshed. As you exhale, breathe out any stress or anxiety you may be feeling.

Think back to the most meaningful success you've had with this organization, and imagine the people you think benefited the most from that success. Imagine that you are speaking with them right now. Ask them what impact your work had on their lives. Ask them if they have any message you can bring back to the rest of the group gathered here that would help us do the work we're planning to do. Once they've shared that message with you, thank them and say goodbye.

Now think of someone who may have the most to gain from the work we'll do together today. Imagine you are speaking with them. Ask them what message they have for us as we start our time together. Once they've shared that message with you, thank them and say goodbye.

Now I invite you to call to mind someone who for you personifies wisdom, someone who wants the best for you and for those you serve. It could be a religious figure; it could be a dear relative; it could be a friend or mentor you have now or that you've had in the past. Ask them what message they have for us today. What insight can they offer us that may guide our work toward the best possible outcomes?

When you're ready, I invite you to come back into the room, open your eyes, and write down any messages you've gotten through this exercise on the sheet of paper in front of you.

Take your time during the visualization. If participants are imagining having conversations with people, allow time for them to have those conversations. This much silence may feel awkward to you as the facilitator, but it is required for the exercise to be successful.

Further, speaking slowly and allowing silence will allow time for the more recalcitrant participants to relax enough to give it a try. Don't let your anxiety rush you to the point that you deprive participants of a meaningful experience. Typically, the guided visualization itself will take around ten full minutes.

Do not assume that participants will see you as a "New Age" quack just because you ask them to close their eyes and visualize something. You may find that many participants have used similar techniques in yoga classes, meditation groups, or even college sports (i.e., visualizing a race before it happens).

Once participants have made notes about their visualizations, ask them to pair up (form a group of three if necessary) and spend two to five minutes sharing what they experienced.

Sharing with a partner allows participants to clarify their insight and get validation from someone else who experienced the unconventional activity.

Then ask the full group to share anything that came up for them during the visualization. You may need to wait a while before someone speaks up, but trust that someone will eventually say something. Even if they say, "That really didn't work for me," or "I thought that was silly," at least they're sharing their experience. In most cases, someone else will respond, "Actually, I found that really helpful." And then they can share why.

Avoid drawing any conclusions from this discussion. Remember, the purpose of this exercise is simply to ground participants (individually and as a group) to deepen the work they will do later. Facilitate meaningful sharing, and then move on.

5. CONTENT INTRODUCTION

By this point, you have welcomed, introduced, oriented, and grounded the group. Now it is time to dig into the topics of the day. Your approach will vary based on whether the key information participants need comes from an outside source (including you) or from one another.

5.1 Fishbowl Exercise

If participants need to hear from one another – e.g., if the workshop objectives relate to their internal dynamics – then this "fishbowl" exercise taught to me by my mentor Marty Goldberg is a fantastic choice.

It is called a "fishbowl" because the group gets to listen quietly to a conversation among a subset of its members who share a similar point of view, much like a group of people watching a fish swim in a fishbowl. The group sits in an outer circle of chairs, while those having the conversation pull their chairs into the middle.

Because they are not actively participating in the conversations they observe, those seated in the outer circle actually listen to what is being said. They are not busy formulating what they will say in response, as they would be in a typical debate or discussion.

Start by asking the subgroup with the most authority or power (e.g., Board Chair and CEO, or CEO and executive team) to have a conversation among themselves in the middle of the circle, while the rest of the group listens in. Give them a set of questions designed around the key topics for the workshop, such as:

- *What are the biggest opportunities and challenges you see facing this organization?*
- *What's working well on this team, and what is holding us back?*
- *What do you see in the group's strategic context that others may not know about?*

Once this group has completed their conversation (about eight to ten minutes), ask them to rejoin the outer circle and invite the next "rung" of the hierarchy to move to the middle to have a conversation of their own. When they finish, invite the next rung, and so on.[2]

Allow roughly the same amount of time for each group. Groups from lower echelons of the organization likely will have more people, but each typically will have less desire to speak their mind than those at the top, so giving roughly equal time to each group works just fine.

By starting with those with the most power, you give them an opportunity to model openness and honesty for the rest of the group so that others are not afraid to speak their true opinions. Tell the leaders prior to the workshop that this is a role you expect them to play.

You can also use this exercise with a group of peers that divide into opposing groups along several dimensions, such as age, size of organization, or urban/rural.

The magic of this exercise is that it gives all participants a holistic view of what is going on for the group or organization – integrating all perspectives present – within a short period of time. Participants hear the other perspectives because they are actually listening; they are not just formulating their response.

After the last subgroup's conversation, have them rejoin the outer circle and ask the full group what stood out for them across

---

2. Use your best judgment when you are working with groups that don't fit into a strict hierarchy. For example, with a nonprofit membership association's board of directors, I had the groups enter the "fishbowl" in the following order: board chair and CEO, the rest of the board's executive committee, the rest of the board, staff, and invited guests.

all of the "fishbowl" conversations. Do not draw any final conclusions, but give participants a chance to highlight any new understandings they have gained.

Then form mixed groups (ideally five to eight people, with at least one person from each "fishbowl" subgroup) and instruct the groups to discuss a certain question based on what they heard in the "fishbowl," such as:

- *What three strategies seem most promising for the organization to pursue in the next three years?*
- *What three initiatives should we start in order to address the issues facing the organization?*

CREATING A "FISHBOWL"
WHENEVER PEOPLE ARE NOT LISTENING

Organization leaders often hire facilitators because the organization's teams cannot seem to have the conversations they need to have without one. This is because when people disagree, they stop listening. When one person is speaking, the other person is busy planning how they will refute what is being said. You can interrupt this pattern anytime people disagree by using the underlying principle of the "fishbowl" exercise, which is that like-minded people have a conversation among themselves, while other people just listen. Then they switch.

If you find participants talking over one another, call a "facilitator's timeout" and do a quick poll to create groups around each relevant point of view. Instruct each group to have a short conversation with the others listening in. Intervene swiftly if any listener starts talking out of turn. After hearing from all groups, invite anyone to share a synthesizing statement that addresses everything they have heard. In most cases, a few things will happen. First, the full group will discover that the issue is more nuanced than they had thought. Second, participants will express underlying beliefs that they have never said aloud before, since someone is finally listening. These beliefs may be hard for some to hear, but at least they reveal where people really stand on the issue. While this "fishbowl" discussion will not necessarily resolve the disagreement, it will likely clear the air and help people understand where and how to move forward together.

5.2 Expert Presentation

For some groups, the information they need to have the conversations the workshop requires will come from an external source – perhaps you, perhaps another expert.

Examples might include:

- The results of an individual assessment like the Myers-Briggs Type Indicator.
- The results of an assessment of the group's dynamics.
- A framework or tool they can apply to improve their performance, like Marshall Rosenberg's Nonviolent Communication framework.[3]
- A methodology for the specific task at hand, such as strategic planning.
- A thought-provoking report or framework, such as a trend analysis or a set of future scenarios.

Over time, you will develop your repertoire of ideas and presentations to help the groups you facilitate.

Sometimes you or the client will want to invite another expert to present to the group at this point in the workshop. Make sure you understand what the presenter will say, and that it fits into the overall process you are designing. If possible, talk directly to the expert presenter in advance. Pay attention to their overall attitude toward the presentation. If they have a firm point of view, are pitching a product, or tend to "get into the weeds"

3 See *Nonviolent Communication: A Language of Life* by Marshall B. Rosenberg.

of their topic without understanding participants' operating context, then develop a plan to neutralize their biases, keep them on task, and prevent them from derailing the workshop.

Be wary of facilitating the discussion of their content if it is unfamiliar to you, or if you do not see its relevance to the workshop's overall objectives (but the client insists on including it). Instead, ask someone from the client's organization to facilitate that segment, and shift into a timekeeper role. Otherwise, you will likely take the blame for a discussion that may contribute little to the group's success.

Alternatively, replace the discussion with a brief question-and-answer period with the expert, which you facilitate by keeping time and calling on participants to ask their questions. That might suffice as a discussion of the expert's content, and then you can move on with the other activities you have planned.

With so much content available online, you may decide to use a video, article, or some other off-the-shelf resource to present new ideas to the group, either during the workshop or as preparation ahead of time. If you send something out in advance, at least be sure to present it briefly during the workshop, since some participants may not have read it.

Whether the content comes from you, another expert, or an online resource, form the appropriate groups of participants and ask them to have the relevant conversations. For example, if using the Myers-Briggs Type Indicator, it makes sense to have those with similar Myers-Briggs types explore their similarities. If using future scenarios, form a different group around each scenario and have them explore their scenario's strategic implications for the organization. If using an expert presentation, ask the small groups to brainstorm how the organization might apply what they have just learned. Whatever form it takes, allow people to engage with new ideas in small-group discussions as a way to deepen their learning.

6. HARVESTING INSIGHTS

Let the small groups report their insights to the full group to find the key areas of convergence and divergence that will likely become the focus of the rest of the workshop. Be careful, though; many report-outs drain the group's energy as a participant reads every word on a flip-chart or gives a play-by-play account of their small group's conversation. As the facilitator, you will need to state your expectations for the report-out.

Tell participants that you would like to hear from each group, but you are only interested in three or four highlights from their discussion, like big insights or new initiatives. Tell them how much time each small group will have to present. Ask them not to spend their time on ideas that other groups have already shared, other than to note that their group discussed it too. (It helps to give these instructions as the small-group discussions come to a close so that those reporting out know how to prepare.)

Playfully ask, "Who had the biggest insight and wants to share it right away?" Let the group that volunteers do most or all of their report-out, but then keep things moving by shifting attention to another group. Be ready to interject to keep the report-out moving if a participant starts belaboring the same point. Say, "This is great, but we have limited time to hear from all of the groups. What are the key points we need to know to move forward?"

After each group has reported out, facilitate a full-group discussion of what participants shared. Admittedly, full-group discussions like this may frighten first-time facilitators. Your role in full-group facilitations is three-fold. First, get people talking. Second, redirect the conversation if it moves in a direction that does not serve the group or its objectives. Third, keep track of time.

To get the group talking, ask open-ended questions that invite participants to share their thoughts on the topic. An open-ended question invites an infinite set of answers and generates

even deeper questions and explorations. For example, "What was most valuable to you about that exercise?" or "What concerns do you have about adopting the proposed strategy?" By contrast, a closed question has a limited set of possible answers, as in, "Did you like that exercise?" or "Do you think you should adopt that strategy?"

Any open-ended question relevant to the topic likely will get people talking, in part because many follow the politician's adage: If you don't like the question, answer the question you wanted instead. However, I tend to ask questions that highlight the convergence and divergence around the topic.

For convergence, ask, "Are there ideas that several of the small groups had in common?" Those ideas may easily transition into forward motion. For divergence, ask, "What really surprised you about what you heard?" or "Does anyone have a perspective that is quite different from what was just shared?" These questions surface divergent opinions that can enhance the group's overall understanding of the topic.

Once participants are talking, your job is to attune yourself completely to the tone and energy of the conversation – moment by moment, word by word – so that you can redirect it as soon as it drifts off topic in a way that does not serve the group or their objectives for the workshop. Note the use of the word "or" in that sentence: sometimes the conversation serves the group but not the objectives, for example, by surfacing conflicting belief systems of which the client has previously been unaware.

This is both the easiest and the hardest part of facilitation – easy because you as the facilitator may not have to *do* very much, and hard because you must be completely attentive to the conversation in every moment and measure what is being said against your own internal "tuning fork" to determine whether or not it is serving the group.

As a general guide, here are a few ways the conversation may drift off topic, and how you can intervene to redirect it:

- A participant gets stuck in a loop where they keep making the same point over and over again. Intervene by summarizing what they have said, asking them if you've captured the main points, and then asking if other participants have other thoughts to share. If necessary, remind the group of the question you originally posed.

- A participant shares a point of view they have shared many times before, in the same words and with the same effect. As mentioned in the previous bullet, intervene by summarizing the key points and checking them with the speaker. Then ask if there's anything else they would like to say so they can feel heard on this issue, and give them a few minutes to speak. Confirm they have fully expressed their view, and ask participants if they have heard it. Then move on to someone else. (If they later return to the same point with no new information, remind them that the group has already heard that perspective and they do not need to keep saying it.)

- A participant goes off on an enthusiastic diatribe about a new insight they have had that is only tangentially related to the current topic. Intervene by sharing as much excitement about their insight as you can, and then note that it is not immediately germane to the current topic. Ask them to articulate the insight in a phrase or two that can be captured on a flip-chart for further exploration after the workshop.

- Two participants or groups of participants get locked in an argument that does not deepen anyone's understanding of the issue at hand. Intervene by creating a mini "fishbowl" exercise that allows both parties to share their perspective without interruption. (See box on page 74.) Then ask the full group about the implications of those divergent perspectives for their actions going forward, e.g., "What should we do with the different opinions on this issue?"

- A participant expresses an opinion that apparently no one else in the room shares, and an awkward silence falls over the group. Intervene by asking a question that expands the perspective offered by the speaker to include at least one other participant. For example, "Who else has concerns about the direction we've been headed thus far?" or "What other stakeholders may share that opinion?" The purpose here is simply to reestablish the coherence of the group by validating *something* about what the participant has shared, even if no one else in the room shares their actual opinion.

- People exhaust the current topic or run out of energy. Intervene by asking another open-ended question. Your initial question may not have probed beyond the group's existing agreement. Alternatively, ask the group if they want to take a break, and then plan to resume the conversation at a deeper level once they return.

Your last responsibility in the full-group discussion is to watch the time. Remember, this conversation is just one part of a longer process you have planned. Manage the pace so that participants can explore all relevant issues without running over the time allowed.

Intervene as appropriate throughout the discussion to keep participants moving through the topic, e.g., "This seems like an important issue, but I know there are other important issues we have yet to address. Have we said enough about this one issue for now so we can move on? Who has another relevant issue they would like to raise?"

When the time comes to wrap up the discussion, ask if anyone has any final thoughts on the topic that they have not yet shared and that they can state in a sentence or two. Allow one or two people to do so, but cut off the discussion when it is time to move on. You can offer a synthesizing statement of your own to tie together the various points made during the discussion, or you can ask the group to do so – e.g., "Who can make a synthesizing statement to capture the key points from this discussion that we will need to remember as we move forward?"

If the small-groups' flip-chart pages are organized and legible, post them together on the wall as a visual record of the outbound trip. Write any highlights from the facilitated discussion on a new flip-chart page.

This concludes the outbound trip. The group starts in *thought* by orienting themselves to the objectives, agenda, agreements, and topic for the day. They access their *emotion* through introductions, grounding, and small-group discussions. They arrive in *intuition* where they develop a more holistic understanding and likely find a few intimations of how to proceed. Then it is time to translate those intimations into clear frameworks for action that will guide them forward, which will be the work of the inbound trip.

A SIMPLE GUIDE TO FLIP-CHARTING

Follow these rules to be successful at flip-charting without a degree from art school.

1. Use chisel tip permanent markers. Test them before the workshop begins to ensure they have not dried up. If possible, bring your own.
2. Take two markers to the flip-chart – one cool, one warm:
   a. Write text in cool colors: black, blue, dark green, or dark purple.
   b. Accent your text (underlines, bullet points, circles) with a warm color, like red or orange.
   c. Never write on a flip-chart in yellow.
3. Write clearly in large letters that all participants can read.
4. As you write distinct ideas or separate bullet points, draw a line completely across the page after each one. This clarifies the locations of separations.
5. When you continue the same topic on a new flip-chart page, add the same heading and number the pages so you can put them in order when gathering the workshop outputs.
6. Bend your knees as you need to write lower on the flip-chart. If you just bend at the waist, it's likely that you'll end up writing your lines of text in a descending fashion, as well as sticking your rear end out at the participants.

Because this marks an important stopping point, you may want to break for lunch in a full-day workshop. Alternatively, you can schedule lunch before the report-out if that timing works better. In that case, the unresolved issues from the small-group discussions will likely show up in the lunch conversations, which might generate new ideas to be shared later. But in nearly all cases, the small-group discussions – the heart of the outbound trip – should occur before lunch, and before the post-lunch "food coma" sets in.

4

The Inbound Trip:
From *Intuition* to *Thought*

NOW THE GROUP MUST TRANSLATE the insights it obtained on the outbound trip into tangible constructs that will guide its action beyond the workshop. This is the work of the inbound trip. See the design flowchart for the inbound trip on the next page.

7. PLANNING ACTIVITY

Depending on the workshop's objectives, you may need multiple rounds of the following planning activities. If your objective is to identify promising strategic initiatives that warrant further research by the organization's staff, then one round may suffice. If your objective is to develop detailed timelines, then you may need multiple rounds for identifying, planning, and scheduling the different areas of effort. In that case, you could use the same

Design Flowchart for the "Inbound Trip"

From "Outbound Trip"

What is most important for this round of planning?

Reach high level of detail

Capture everyone's input

7.1. Traditional Breakout Discussion

7.2. Rotational Exercise

Is another round of planning required?

Yes

No

8. Full Group (Open) Discussion

9. Next Steps / Commitments

10. Evaluation

11. Gratitudes

Adjourn

technique multiple times, or you could mix it up by using a variety of techniques.

In any event, be wary of keeping groups in a planning mode for long periods of time. Match the scale of the planning to do on the inbound trip to the scale of insight you expect to capture on the outbound trip.

7.1 Traditional Breakout Discussion

Form small groups of five to eight participants and ask them to answer a focused question related to the workshop's objectives and to what the activity seeks to plan, such as:

- *What statements are you absolutely certain will be true in five years if this team is successful?*
- *What processes, practices, or systems do we need to put in place to help this team collaborate more effectively?*
- *What activities need to be completed to effect your assigned strategy?*
- *What are the key milestones along the way?*

You can assign these groups in a few ways. First, you can assign people to specific groups or topics if you want to bring certain expertise to bear or if you want certain participants to work together (or not to). Second, you can invite participants to self-organize around the topics that interest them, while making sure the groups are roughly equal in size. Third, you can use a hybrid approach of letting participants self-organize, but setting rules on the diversity of each group (e.g., at least one person from each department). It may be helpful to hold off on assigning the topics to the groups until after the groups are formed, so that participants do not slow down the process by "gaming the system" to get on the group to which you have assigned their favorite topic.

7.2 Rotational Exercise

This unique planning activity will quickly generate a shared commitment to a set of high-priority strategies or initiatives.

Set up three (or more) flip-charts around the room. Divide participants into groups using one of the methods described earlier: assigned, self-organizing, or hybrid. Ask each group to assemble around one of the flip-charts.

Ask each group to choose a "scribe" – someone to capture the discussion in reasonable detail on the flip-chart. This scribe has an important role.

Assign a topic to each flip-chart. This could be an existing framework with broad categories of activity (e.g., structure, culture, and systems), or it could be the top three ideas to emerge on the outbound trip. You just need a framework that usefully differentiates the work you expect each group to do. If you have not quite named a topic properly, trust that participants will correct it in the course of their small-group work.

FACILITATOR'S ROLE DURING
SMALL-GROUP EXERCISES

The small-group exercises are not the facilitator's break time. You should wander around to listen in on each group. Give them additional guidance if they are not following the instructions the way you anticipated. Push them to think in a different direction if they seem stuck in familiar conversations.

But don't say more than you have to. Some facilitators love to engage with the small groups, but in my opinion, this often subverts the ownership participants are starting to feel over the discussion. Avoid interventions that are intended to show off your expertise. As my mentor Zigy Kaluzny says, ask yourself: Does this need to be said, or do I need to say it?

While this is not your break time, you may decide to refill your coffee or water or even use the restroom while the small groups are working. To some extent, your stepping away from the small groups for a moment communicates that you trust them to do the work. Only do this after you are sure they understand the instructions, and never leave the room for more than a couple minutes in case participants have questions along the way.

Each group spends some time (usually fifteen to twenty minutes) addressing their topic. After this time, everyone in the group *except for the scribe* rotates to the next topic. The scribe stays behind to brief the group rotating into the topic on what the first group discussed. This brief should only last two to three minutes.

The incoming group then builds on the previous group's work using a "yes, and" approach. The goal is not to critique what the previous group said, but rather to accept it ("yes") and improve upon it ("and"). Because the exercise accumulates every group's input on each topic, participants become jointly invested in the outputs across all topics. (If any genuine disagreements survive this exercise, they surely will come up in the full-group discussion that follows.)

After working on their current topics, the groups rotate again, receive a brief from the scribe for their new topic, and get back to work. This process repeats itself until all rounds are complete.

This usually means three rounds, three groups, and three topics. This way, every participant (except the scribes) gets to provide input on every topic, so they leave the workshop feeling fully heard and fully invested. With more than three rounds, people may run out of energy before the activity is over. If four or more distinct ideas all warrant further development, consider deferring one or more to a later conversation, or do three rotations but allow participants to self-organize around their preferred topic at the start of each round.

Because the scribe stays at one flip-chart for the entire exercise, choose scribes whose input is not critical across all topics or who will have a later opportunity to contribute their ideas. Staff participating in a board retreat may fit both criteria, for example. If a certain person has direct responsibility for one of the topics, consider assigning them as its scribe so they can hear face-to-face the input they later will be asked to put into practice. If everyone really needs to work on everything, then ask the scribes to follow their original groups after they brief the incoming groups, and ask a different person to act as a scribe in each round.

Divide the amount of time for this exercise roughly into thirds, but give a little more time to the first round since they will be figuring out the process. Also, later groups likely will need a little less time since the earlier groups will have already made many of the key points.

After the last round, ask each scribe to give a quick report-out of the overall discussion on their topic. Since everyone has already worked on each topic, you will likely move quickly to a full-group discussion of cross-topic overlaps, broader implications, and next steps. Harvest this discussion, using a flip-chart if necessary, as preparation for the next step.

PRIORITIZING

During the process of building out ideas, you may need to prune the ideas to keep the group focused on the highest priorities. You can do this in two different ways.

The simplest way to get a group to prioritize the ideas they have generated is to give them each a small number of dot-shaped stickers and invite them to get up and put their dots on the ideas they view as the highest priorities. This works well when the different ideas would require roughly the same amount of time, effort, and investment. If some of the ideas overlap, you may need to work with the group to refine the options by combining or splitting the ideas. Once everyone has had a chance to vote, count up the votes for each idea and work with the group to determine which ideas will be developed moving forward (usually those with the most votes).

If the ideas vary in cost, you can bring that dimension into the prioritization process using a variant of an exercise developed by Luke Hohmann and described in his book, *Innovation Games: Creating Breakthrough Products Through Collaborative Play*. In this exercise, ask the group to assign a total cost to each of the ideas that incorporates labor, money, and any other resources. List these total cost figures as the "price" of each idea. Add up the total price of all ideas, and then make a fraction of that amount (e.g., half) available to the group as a shared budget, equally divided among participants. Participants then wander around the room, negotiating with one another to amass enough money to purchase the ideas they consider most important. Negotiations are required because the total cost of the ideas exceeds the shared budget. For currency, use dot-shaped stickers or fake paper money.

Admittedly, this exercise works best when the cost estimates are roughly accurate, so you may only want to use this approach when the organization's staff has had time to work up the estimates before the workshop. Afternoon cost estimates of the morning's ideas are less likely to yield a meaningful list of priorities.

8. FULL-GROUP (OPEN) DISCUSSION

After the planning, leave time (approximately thirty minutes) for full-group discussion of the planning outputs as well as any other concerns that have yet to be addressed. This discussion reinforces the sense that it's "their meeting" and prevents participants from leaving the workshop feeling like they did not have a chance to speak their mind. Further, including this discussion in the agenda creates a buffer in case one of the earlier exercises runs over.

9. NEXT STEPS/COMMITMENTS

Tell the group what you as the facilitator will do following the workshop, such as typing up flip-charts and writing a workshop summary. Tell them what that process will look like, what the timeline will be, and what expectations you have of them.

If you will have a limited role after the workshop, ask someone from the client organization to collect any flip-charts, templates, or notes, and advise them on how they might compile those outputs for optimal value to the group.

After discussing these next steps, invite participants to share any next steps they will take, or that they would like someone else (even you) to take. This is an opportunity to ensure that their good efforts during the workshop provide lasting value. You may not always know what that looks like, so ask. If a participant asks you to do something that is outside the scope of your engagement, say so, or make a note of it for a subsequent discussion with the client to determine if and how it will be accomplished.

You also may ask participants what commitments they would like to make. Give them a few minutes to write something down, then invite them to share with the full group. In some cases, the client may require this activity so they can hold people accountable for moving forward on the initiatives coming out of the workshop.

However, I am generally skeptical about the commitments participants make at this point in the workshop. They have been working hard for most of the day, and many will need time to reflect on what has been said before they can commit to specific actions or changes in behavior. For this reason, capture participants' commitments on a flip-chart or in your own notes but provide them later to the client in a form that does not feel "set in stone." Allow participants to refine them once they have had a chance to reflect on the workshop. Alternatively, ask participants to write their commitments on self-addressed postcards that you can send to them after the workshop for further consideration.

10. EVALUATION

To my mind, the measure of a workshop's success is whether or not the group accomplishes its objectives. That said, many clients will request an evaluation of some sort, and you, too, may want to know what worked and what didn't so that you can hone your craft. Further, if you will facilitate the same group again in the future, you certainly don't want to keep doing things they don't like.

You can do an evaluation in a few different ways:

- Provide a hard copy evaluation form and ask participants to fill it out before they leave. I typically include a six-point rating scale (an even number so a participant cannot just mark the middle) for the workshop's key dimensions (e.g., design, facilitation, and logistics), as well as a few open-ended questions about what went well and what could be improved. The advantage of a hard copy, real-time questionnaire is that more participants will complete it, but the answers may be of lower quality, for example, if they are rushing to get somewhere.

- Provide an online survey that participants can complete after the workshop. The questions may be the same as those listed for the hard copy evaluation. With an online survey, you will likely get fewer responses, but the answers may be of higher quality.

- Conduct a public, real-time assessment by asking participants to raise one, two, three, four, or five fingers to rate the workshop. A former colleague of mine always got a cheap laugh by reminding people, if they were giving one figure, to make sure it was their index finger (and not their middle). Then ask those who gave fives and ones to share why. Alternatively, draw a vertical line on a flip-chart and make one side with a plus sign and the other with a minus sign. Ask participants what worked and what didn't work about the workshop, and capture their comments on the flip-chart.

Some participants conduct rather elaborate evaluations at the end of a workshop. I see the value of this, but at the same time, I

wonder if it shifts too much attention to the facilitator and their process and away from the group. For this reason, I suggest that you get through whatever evaluation you choose as quickly as possible, and then move on to the "gratitudes" as described here.

11. GRATITUDES

End the workshop by giving participants an opportunity to express gratitude for a person, thing, or opportunity related to the work they have done together. Do not make this a mandatory exercise where you go around the circle and participants have to come up with something to say.

Instead, open up the space for gratitude by inviting participants to speak if the spirit moves them. Model for them what this gratitude will look like – for example, "I'd like to thank Richard for setting up all the logistics for this workshop. It made my job a lot easier." Then sit quietly and let people speak if they would like.

People in organizations rarely dedicate time to expressing gratitude for one another. This way of ending the workshop brings people together simply by letting them share their positive feelings for each other. Also, it ends the workshop on a positive note and smooths out any feathers ruffled in heated discussions throughout the day.

Like the guided visualization discussed earlier, these gratitudes require you to sit quietly for longer than you may like. Trust the process and allow enough time for people to formulate the sentiments they want to share. When you sense that most people who want to speak have already spoken, wrap up the gratitudes with your own thanks for the good work the group has done together.

If appropriate, let the group know how they can contact you in the future. If you are using slides, advance to a "thank you" slide that includes your photo and contact information. Alternatively, place a stack of your business cards on a table by the door and invite participants to take one, or tell them how to find you on your social media platform of choice. Then be sure to turn it over to the client to adjourn the meeting, since they may have something more to say to the group.

DEBRIEF WITH THE CLIENT

After you collect all the templates, flip-charts, and other workshop outputs, sit down with the client, if possible, to debrief the workshop. This is your chance to hear your client's thoughts about the workshop while it is still fresh in their mind, and to identify and assign any next steps. If you are facilitating a multi-day workshop, do this at the end of each day to take stock of how things are going and to make any necessary changes to the following day's agenda.

Once you have debriefed with the client and packed up all the workshop outputs (or delivered them to the client's safe hands), you are done for the day. Relax, unwind, and celebrate your success. No matter what happened in the workshop, chances are you helped the group have conversations they otherwise would not have had, and you added to your own experience as a facilitator.

5

Facilitating During the Workshop

THE WHOLE MIND WORKSHOP DESIGN presented here will work in the vast majority of situations. But *how* you facilitate a group through this design also matters. If you remember that facilitation is just hanging out with people and helping them solve a problem, you will not be too far off track. This chapter provides more insight into what this looks like in practice.

FOCUS ON THE OBJECTIVES, NOT ON THE AGENDA

You designed an agenda as a tool for helping the group accomplish its objectives, based on what you knew at the time. During the workshop, you will learn more, and you may need to modify the agenda you so painstakingly prepared.

You can take steps to give yourself this flexibility during the workshop. First, do not over-plan the agenda. Avoid clever theatrics and complex logistics in your choice of activities. In my experience, the more complex the activity, the less likely it is to work as anticipated, and by the time you reach that point in the agenda, it may not meet the group's needs anyway. Every group is different; what worked for you before may not work today. By keeping the agenda simple, you give yourself many more degrees of freedom in the facilitation.

For the discussions that will take place throughout the workshop, try to have relevant questions ready in your "back pocket." But recognize that even those questions may become irrelevant as the group surfaces more critical issues that need to be addressed. Further, as you create a safe space for participants to engage with one another, they will raise their own questions for the group to consider.

Granted, some clients – particularly in fear-based organizational cultures – will want to know moment-by-moment what will happen in the workshop. For some of my facilitations with government agencies, for example, clients have required finely detailed facilitation plans (of fifteen pages or more!) that must be updated again and again as the workshop approaches. This wastes innumerable hours for both the client and the facilitation team, and exacerbates the animosity among people within the client organization who preferred different versions along the way.

Second, avoid giving participants anything more than a high-level agenda with time slots and broadly descriptive names for each activity. While you may have provided the client with details of the activities you plan to use, write a participant agenda that removes this detail and instead uses general terms like "Timeline Exercise," "Breakout Exercise," and "Full-Group Discussion." The participant agenda should articulate the rhythm of the day without committing you to specific exercises that ultimately may not serve the group.

Third, tell participants you are willing to change the agenda, and – if appropriate – invite them to tell you when they think the activities you have planned are not helping them achieve their objectives. When they take you up on your offer, be grateful for their honesty and come up with something more useful to do, either from your repertoire or based on input from the group. Of course, always involve the client in any decision to change the agenda, either in a break time conversation or by soliciting their agreement within the full group, depending on the hierarchical structure within the group.

BE IN IT WITH THEM

You may never see this group again after the workshop, but during the workshop, consider yourself as one of them – that is, a member of the team working together to solve their problem. Reflect this orientation in your speech: talk about what "we" will do today to accomplish "our" objectives.

This may seem inconsistent with the notion that "it's their meeting." But what gives you power as a facilitator is that you are genuinely "one of them," but without having any self-interest other than a desire for the group to achieve its objectives. If you are not "one of them," then you may very well have priorities other than their success, such as being seen as clever or skilled. It is by submerging your identity into the group that you gain the ability to help the group.

For example, being part of the group (but without any self-interest) allows you to add value simply by describing what you see happening. If it seems to you that the white men in the group are doing most of the talking, say so. Ask if that is what the group wants, or if they would prefer something different. If you think the exercise you are facilitating is not serving them well, say so. Ask if they share your opinion or if they are making progress.

Since you are one of them, use their language. Avoid trying to translate their statements into your preferred terms and frameworks. Too many facilitators derail the discussion by trying to explain how a participant's comment aligns with some theory they know rather than letting the comment stand for itself. As noted in Chapter 1, the frameworks of greatest value to a group are those that emerge from their own understanding and experience.

If you are one of them, then you can ask them to help you out, too. For example, if you reach the end of a productive discussion but you are not sure how to wrap it up, ask if anyone can offer a good synthesizing statement to capture the key points. If you are at a loss as to what activity or conversation would best serve the group in that moment, ask if anyone has any ideas. Participants are smart, too, and they often know what they need.

And they will tell you, even if you do not listen at first! I once facilitated a group that was rife with interpersonal conflict but ultimately needed to revise its bylaws. I had designed a workshop to address the interpersonal dynamics and explore the issues surrounding the bylaws, but I suspected that voting on actual revisions would take more time than we had available. When several participants asked to do so, I resisted at first, and relented only when I realized the numbers were not in my favor. I told them I was concerned about the time and asked if they thought they could finish within forty-five minutes. They said they could. And they did! Because I saw myself as one of them, I could enjoy their success without feeling like a failure because I had tried to steer them in another direction.

At some point, you will no longer be one of them, so shift your language when you discuss the next steps at the end of the workshop. Distinguish between what you will do and what the group will do to move the workshop's outcomes forward. Otherwise, the group may implicitly assign you more of that burden than you intend to carry.

(BE WILLING TO) MAKE MISTAKES

If you focus on the objectives above all else and view yourself as a full member of the group, then you probably are going to make mistakes – and that's a good thing. There's an authenticity in making mistakes, since we all do it. In fact, early in my facilitation career, I discovered that some of my most successful facilitations (in the sense of the group achieving their objectives) were those in which I had made silly mistakes early on. It may be counterintuitive, but making mistakes (assuming you are focused on objectives and really in it with them) creates a safe space for participants to engage more actively despite their own fear that they will make a mistake.

FACILITATE WITH YOUR BODY

Like actors or dancers, facilitators use their bodies in their performance. Where you position yourself and how you hold your body will influence the energy of the participants and the tone of the discussion. One of the reasons I prefer a circle of chairs as a room setup is because it affords me maximum flexibility in this respect, as opposed to, say, sitting at one end of a boardroom table.

When you stand inside the circle of chairs, for example, you are visibly in control of the room and retain some proportion of everyone's attention, even if someone else is speaking. The speaker knows this and will likely keep their comments short and to the point.

When you take your seat in the circle, you become more of a participant, and the other participants feel freer to speak without asking your permission. The conversation evolves organically, but you are still in a position to impose order or shift the focus if necessary.

When you stand outside the circle, you convey your trust in a group that has taken ownership of the work they are doing together. This might be appropriate during the report-out from a planning activity late in the process, when participants are tending to technical details beyond your level of understanding.

Your gestures will also influence the energy of the workshop. Consider the different gestures shown below:

You may steeple your fingers (A) to indicate confidence as you close off a lively discussion to move on to the next activity. You may put your hands on your hips (B) to let a rambling participant know that you are running out of patience and would like them to wrap up. You may clasp your hands in front of your body (C) in order to remain standing in front of the group without assuming all of the power that posture carries with it. You may even slouch against the wall (D) when the group has productively taken control of the meeting and really does not need you anymore, at least for the time being.

These positions and gestures – and many others – give you a huge nonverbal vocabulary for facilitating the workshop without even saying a word. For example, if you are seated around the circle and you stand up, put your hands on your hips, and walk toward the person who is speaking, there is a good chance they will wrap up their comments pretty quickly! Conversely, if you stand up and leave the circle altogether, the speaker likely will feel emboldened to elaborate on their point of view, and then other participants likely will chime in on their own. Facilitating with your body offers a powerful tool for shaping the conversation to help a group achieve their objectives.

MAKE A FEW REALLY GOOD DECISIONS

Great facilitation typically comes down to making a few good and timely decisions, and going in, you do not know what they will be. Maybe the group will need you to pivot to help them resolve an unexpected issue and get them back on track. Maybe they will need you to say out loud that one of the participants' behavior is impeding meaningful discussion, and to ask that participant to behave differently. Maybe you will need to set up a quick "fishbowl" to help disputing colleagues hear each other for the first time. Maybe you will need to confront a group that does not seem to care about the objectives it has set for itself. Any of these decisions could make or break a facilitation.

I divided the "Whole Mind" workshop design into an "outbound trip" and an "inbound trip," reminiscent of the "hero's journey" Joseph Campbell found in hero myths from all over the world. A great workshop is a journey of self-discovery for the group you are facilitating, but it is also a journey of self-discovery for you as the facilitator.

If there is not a point in the workshop when you genuinely do not know what to do, then it could be you are not pushing the group and yourself hard enough. You may be going through the motions. Great workshops change people, but that change does not come easy. And when you plan a workshop, you do not know what struggles the group will need to overcome. When those struggles emerge, they become your struggles, and you often will have to dig deep to make it through.

Trust yourself in the struggle. If you have an intuition of a way forward, take a risk and give it a try. Or call a break to get yourself centered again. Or chat with the client to get their ideas on how to proceed. Or tell the group that you do not know what to do next, and ask if they have any ideas.

All of these actions take courage, and it is courage that makes for a great facilitator.

You now have all the knowledge you need to facilitate great workshops that change people, organizations, and the world. All that remains is to hone your craft through experience, so go get started. Remember, facilitation is just working with a group of people to help them tackle a difficult problem. If you stay focused on that purpose, you will find success as a facilitator.

Before we adjourn, I'd like to express my gratitude for the pioneers, mentors, and colleagues who have shared with me their art and craft of facilitation, including Marvin Weisbord, Sandra Janoff, Marty Goldberg, Bruce Peters, Emily Oehler, Stacy Tselekis, Doug Krug, Les Wallace, Oliver Markley, Luke Hohmann, Zigy Kaluzny, and Jonathan Peck. I'd also like to thank Emily Oehler, Mark Baker, Panos Smyrnios, and my parents for reading the manuscript and offering insightful feedback.

And with that, we're adjourned!

APPENDIX

Facilitating the Whole Mind ... Online

Ironically, I wrote this book during the COVID-19 pandemic in the spring of 2020, when very few groups in the U.S. were meeting in person. In fact, I had time to write the book largely because many of my workshop facilitations had been canceled in order to minimize transmission of the virus.

As I write, people working from home meet most frequently over the phone or by video conference. Thus, it seems timely to offer guidance on how to translate this book's facilitation approach from in-person workshops to the online or virtual environment.

Admittedly, it is difficult to achieve the workshop experience described in this book using currently available technologies. If a session held in a small room with low ceilings, no windows, and a fixed wooden table in the middle cannot really be called a "workshop," as I suggested earlier, then how much more so for a group of people talking to each other through their computer screens.

Someday in the future, virtual workshops may achieve the same quality of experience as in-person. Virtual reality (VR) or holography may allow people to interact remotely as fully embodied human beings communicating both verbally and nonverbally. (Of course, such technologies may also reduce authenticity, for example, if people take on "avatars" representing mythical characters or superheroes.)

But those are topics for another day. For now, how can you take what you have learned in this book and apply it to virtual workshops you facilitate?

FACILITATE A LONGER PROCESS

When working virtually, your role as a facilitator expands to include much more logistical planning and participant coaching, from the moment you plan the session until you are confident the group will carry the outputs forward. In many cases, you will need to hold multiple sessions.

First, while a workshop could easily last a full day or more, virtual sessions become painful after around ninety minutes, or perhaps two hours if there is a break in the middle.

Second, beyond ten or so people, participation declines significantly, since the session feels more like an online presentation than a conversation. Or more typically, such sessions become conversations among the three or four most vocal participants, with others looking on passively (or checking their email).

As a result, what would have been a full-day workshop if held in person could be a series of several online sessions with different sets of participants. In this case, you are not facilitating a workshop so much as you are leading an organizational process designed to meet the objectives the workshop would have achieved.

But the same flow still applies. Engage people in *thought* to figure out how they are conceptualizing the issue and defining the problem. Invite them to connect through *emotion* to figure out what motivations they share and to detach from ways of thinking that are not serving them well. Include time for *intuition* to explore alternative approaches to the problem. Structure activities where they can translate new insights into clear frameworks for moving forward. The process itself does not change. You simply need to set up the process as a longer-term interaction that includes online conversations with fewer participants, separated by individual and small-group activities that move them forward in between.

DO MORE PLANNING FOR VIRTUAL WORKSHOPS

The success of a virtual facilitation depends much more on advance planning than does an in-person workshop. In person, a facilitator can "read the room" and make changes to the agenda "on the fly" when required to help the group achieve its objectives. This becomes more difficult in a virtual session, for two reasons.

First, online you receive less information about how participants are doing and whether or not the activities you've selected are moving them in the right direction. Instead of a room full of human bodies spewing forth nonverbal messages about their conscious and unconscious feelings, you have tiny video feeds showing participants only from the neck up. So you will have very little information on which to base a decision to mix things up.

Second, it is difficult to communicate a change to the agenda to a group of online participants. Invariably, someone's audio will drop off just as you are giving the revised instructions, and they will be confused for the rest of the session.

Thus, you will need to plan a virtual session at a much higher level of detail than you would for an in-person workshop.

As noted earlier, you are designing a process, not a workshop. Separate the work that can be done offline and set up the appropriate activities. Individual activities could include assigned readings or videos, surveys, worksheets, or reflective exercises. Small-group activities could include discussions, projects, or even in-person meetings if subsets of participants are located together.

For each online session, think about where it fits in the process, and what the group will need at that moment. If it's early on, do they need to connect on an emotional and interpersonal level, especially if some have never met face to face? Later on, do they need to work in small groups to address the implications of a big decision they have made together?

Plan out an online session of no more than two hours that includes a mix of activities, shifting every ten to fifteen minutes between full-group discussions, small-group breakouts (many online meeting platforms allow this), videos (no more than fifteen minutes long, and only if there is value in discussing their responses in real time), brief presentations (if the content cannot be provided in advance), conversations with invited experts, and even individual activities. Here again, you can take some risks. Give participants a ten-minute break but ask them to use the time to take a walk outside. Invite participants to sit silently for three minutes to reflect on a particular issue. Lead a guided visualization. You will be surprised how well such activities can work, even over the internet.

Use a set of slides to guide people through the activities. Send these out in advance, or at least at the start of the session (ideally as handouts on which participants can take their own notes), so that you can minimize the amount of time they are showing on the screen. Maximize the time participants spend looking at a human face – yours or someone else's. Also, participants with a copy of the slides can follow along even if they are participating only by audio.

Whether as handouts or on the computer screen, slides will look much smaller than they would when projected onto a full-size screen. So keep them simple. Use meaningful images, not distracting or obnoxious clip art or animations. Keep words to a minimum – usually twenty words per slide, in twenty-point font or higher.

Given the many "moving parts," find one or more people to help you facilitate. For example, ask one person to run the technology, helping participants join the session and sorting out issues with video and audio. Ask another person to monitor the chat function while you are facilitating the session, and to interject any questions they find particularly relevant to the discussion at hand. Being present to the conversation and managing the technology require two different parts of the brain, so divide the work appropriately.

Once you have designed the session, trust that the group will achieve meaningful outcomes. Demonstrate your trust by sustaining your enthusiasm even without nonverbal feedback from participants that your plan is working. You have little room to adjust the plan once the session has started, so you might as well go with what you've got. Trust that the session will serve its purpose – or that you can adjust the process later to get back on track (just as you might adjust the agenda every two hours or so during an in-person workshop).

SET UP THE TECHNOLOGY FOR MAXIMUM NONVERBAL COMMUNICATION

Apart from the potential for technical difficulties, the biggest difference between an online session and an in-person workshop is the amount of information communicated among participants. Again, at some point, we will solve this problem with VR or holographic meeting platforms, but for now, it's still a challenge. Do your best.

For example, ask participants to scoot their chairs back from their desks and computers so everyone can see their torsos as well as their heads. In addition to creating a new channel for nonverbal communication, this will likely keep participants from doing other work during the session, and it might even encourage them to sit up straight and present a more open posture to the camera. This may be the closest you can come to a circle of chairs in a virtual meeting.

If your meeting platform allows a choice of views, encourage participants to select the option that provides the best view of whoever is speaking. For example, at the time of this writing, Zoom allows participants to toggle between a "gallery" view in which they see all participants simultaneously, and a "speaker" view where the speaker occupies the whole field of view. In "speaker" view, participants can more easily connect emotionally with the speaker and what they are saying. When sharing slides, minimize the time participants see the slides and maximize the time they see you.

At the very least, make sure participants can see one another's entire faces. I have been in online meetings where I could only see one of the participants from the chin up, or a participant had the camera pointing at the wall or ceiling. Stress to your participants the importance of seeing one another, and if necessary, ask individual participants to adjust their cameras to make that possible.

RECOGNIZE THAT IT MAY JUST BE A "MEETING"

Much of what you learned in this book you can apply to virtual facilitations, from the overall flow of the outbound and inbound trips to popping into small-group discussions to make sure they are on track. But it still won't be the same.

It is a rare virtual session that truly deserves the name "workshop," as I have used it in this book. Workshops allow people to spend long periods of meaningful time together, focused on achieving important outcomes. By contrast, virtual sessions offer brief experiences together that hopefully move a group through one or two steps in that process. Given the inherent limitations of the virtual environment, you may decide that you are actually facilitating a meeting, not a workshop. That's not necessarily a bad thing; it's just different, and you will have to adjust your expectations.

But even so, try to elevate the experience using what you learned in this book. Be honest with participants about the limitations of meeting virtually, and ask people explicitly not to multitask during the session. Remind them that working together on shared challenges is a blessing, and the fact that they must meet virtually rather than in-person implies that they should work even harder to be fully present to other participants and to the task at hand.

The quality of a workshop is ultimately determined by how well the participants fully engage their *thought*, *emotion*, and *intuition* to achieve their shared outcomes. I have written this book to help you help this to happen. Granted, this is harder to achieve in virtual sessions, but if you set this as a goal, you will likely do the best you can.

The COVID-19 pandemic, which continues as I write, has taught us at least two things about how we work together. First, we have learned how much we can do from home. Second, we have learned how precious our in-person time together is, since we have been forced to go without it. During the recovery from the pandemic and beyond, great facilitation will be as important as ever. Our time together is a real blessing, so it's up to us facilitators to make sure it doesn't go to waste!

About the Author

Eric Meade facilitates workshops for organizations and communities who want to move forward together in new ways. He leads the Whole Mind Strategy Group, a consulting consortium based in Superior, Colorado, and teaches strategic planning at American University in Washington, DC. Eric's previous book, *Reframing Poverty: New Thinking and Feeling About Humanity's Greatest Challenge*, won multiple awards, including a Nautilus Book Award and an Independent Press Award. Visit him at www.wholemindstrategy.com.

About the Illustrator

Lucinda Levine provides dynamic visual support for organizations who want more out of their meetings, workshops, and convenings. Her visual style draws on years of experience as an illustrator and has been called insightful, witty, and thoughtful. Lucinda is founder and principal of Inkquiry Visuals, a full-service graphic recording studio based in Washington, DC. She is a member of the International Forum of Visual Practitioners. Visit her at www.Inkquiryvisuals.com.

Made in the USA
Middletown, DE
02 July 2020

11847891R00071